Top Dogs Run

Written by Samantha Eardley

Collins

The dog can hop.

It is up.

Toss the rag.

4

Can Toff get it?

Dogs run up the hill.

I pat and hug Bill.

Fin pulls and tugs.

Not the sock, Fin!

Pug in a dog bed

back

bed

pads

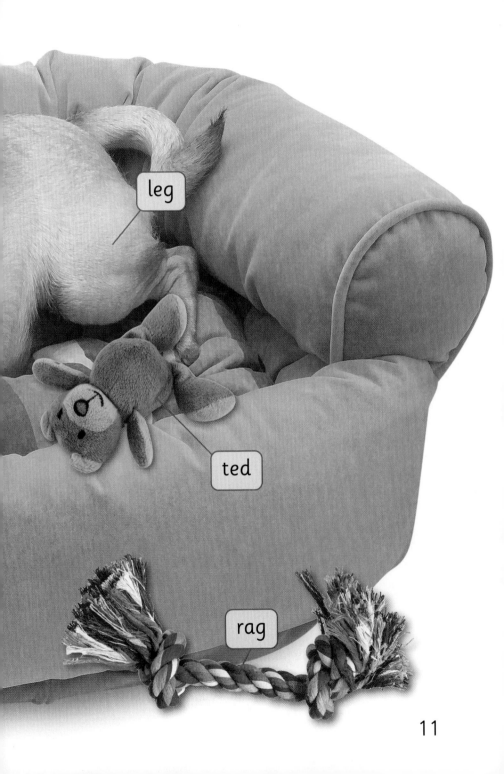

leg

ted

rag

Dogs can ...

get hugs and pats ✔

hop ✔

pull and tug ✔

get rags ✔

run ✔

Top dogs

Review: After reading

Use your assessment from hearing the children read to choose any GPCs, words or tricky words that need additional practice.

Read 1: Decoding
- On page 7, point to **pat** and **hug**. Ask: Do these words have different meanings? Encourage the children to mime patting and hugging a dog to make the meanings clear.
- Point to the word **Dogs** on page 6. Ask the children to sound out each letter then blend. (**D/o/g/s**) Repeat for:

  T/o/ss (page 4)   **g/e/t** (page 5)   **h/i/ll** (page 6)   **t/u/g/s** (page 8)
- Point to **It** on page 3. Say: Can you sound this out silently in your head before reading aloud? Repeat for **up**.

Read 2: Prosody
- Model reading pages 4–7 to the children as if you are a television presenter. Ask the children to read the pages too, encouraging them to use a tone of excitement. Ensure they see the question mark and use a questioning tone for page 5.

Read 3: Comprehension
- Ask the children about the things they've seen dogs do. Where did they see them? Can they describe the dog?
- Look together at the cover and talk about the title. What are **top dogs**? (e.g. *the best dogs*) Talk about the things dogs can do, too. (e.g. *hop, tug*)
- Turn to pages 14 and 15. Encourage the children to recall vocabulary by discussing a caption for each picture. Prompt with a question: What is this dog doing?
- Talk about the actions in relation to other animals: What else runs? (e.g. *hamsters*) Where might they run? (*on a wheel*)
- Bonus content: Turn to pages 12 and 13. Say: Let's see what these dogs can do. Encourage the children to read each caption, followed by "tick". Encourage them to read with confidence, speaking as if they are judges at a dog show.